Tail Toes Eyes Ears Nose

by Marilee Robin Burton

Harper & Row, Publishers

With special thanks to Jerry Jarvis

Tail Toes Eyes Ears Nose
Copyright © 1989 by Marilee Robin Burton
All rights reserved. No part of this book may be
used or reproduced in any manner whatsoever without
written permission except in the case of brief quotations
embodied in critical articles and reviews. Printed in
the United States of America. For information address
Harper & Row Junior Books, 10 East 53rd Street,
New York, N.Y. 10022. Published simultaneously in
Canada by Fitzhenry & Whiteside Limited, Toronto.
Typography by Andrew Rhodes
1   2   3   4   5   6   7   8   9   10
First Edition

Library of Congress Cataloging-in-Publication Data
Burton, Marilee Robin.
  Tail, toes, eyes, ears, nose / by Marilee Robin Burton.—1st ed.
    p.   cm.
  Summary: Presents body parts of eight animals for the reader to
guess what the whole animal looks like.
    ISBN 0-06-020873-2: $
    ISBN 0-06-020874-0 (lib. bdg.): $
    1. Animals—Pictorial works—Juvenile literature.   2. Morphology
(Animals)—Pictorial works—Juvenile literature.   3. Picture
puzzles—Juvenile literature.   [1. Animals—Pictorial works.
2. Morphology (Animals)—Pictorial works.   3. Picture puzzles.]
I. Title.
QL49.B796 1989   87-33276
E—dc19   CIP
                                                              AC

For My Mother

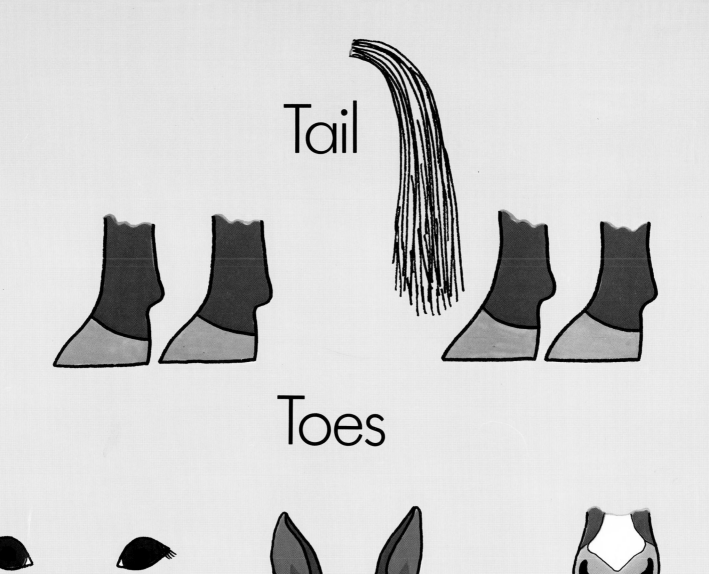

Tail

Toes

Eyes

Ears

Nose

Horse

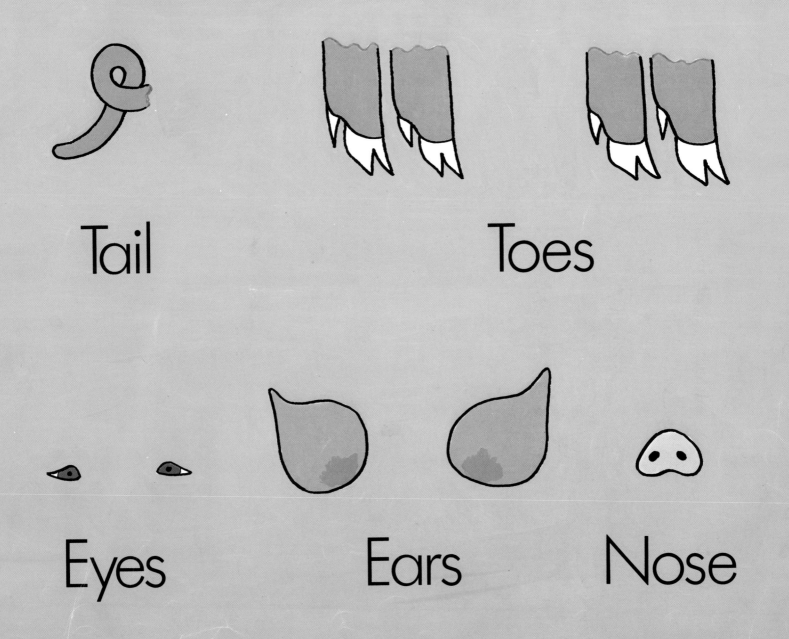

Tail

Toes

Eyes

Ears

Nose

Pig

Tail

Toes   Eyes   Ears   Nose

Mouse

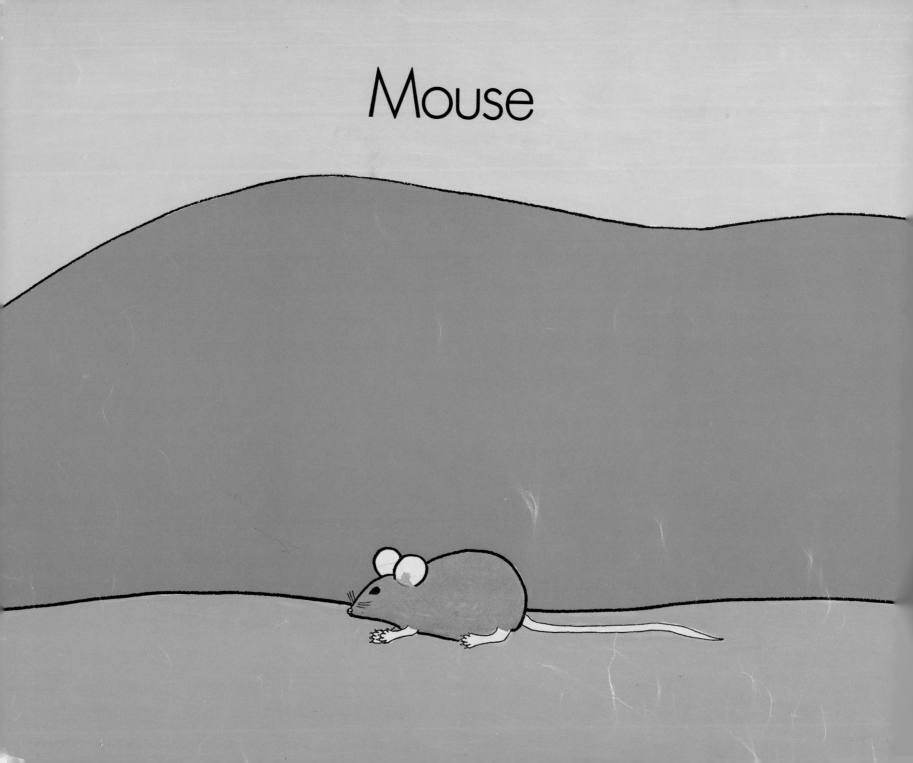

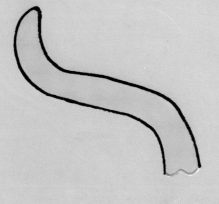

Tail

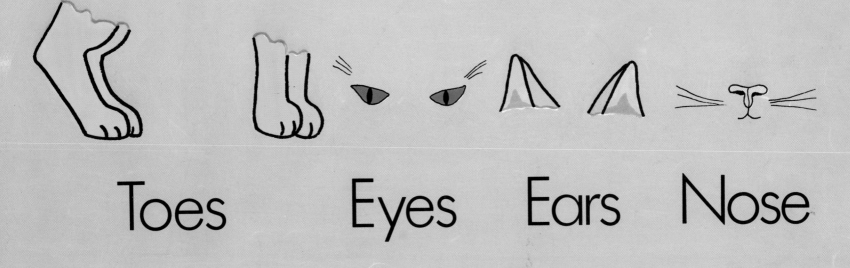

Toes   Eyes   Ears Nose

Cat

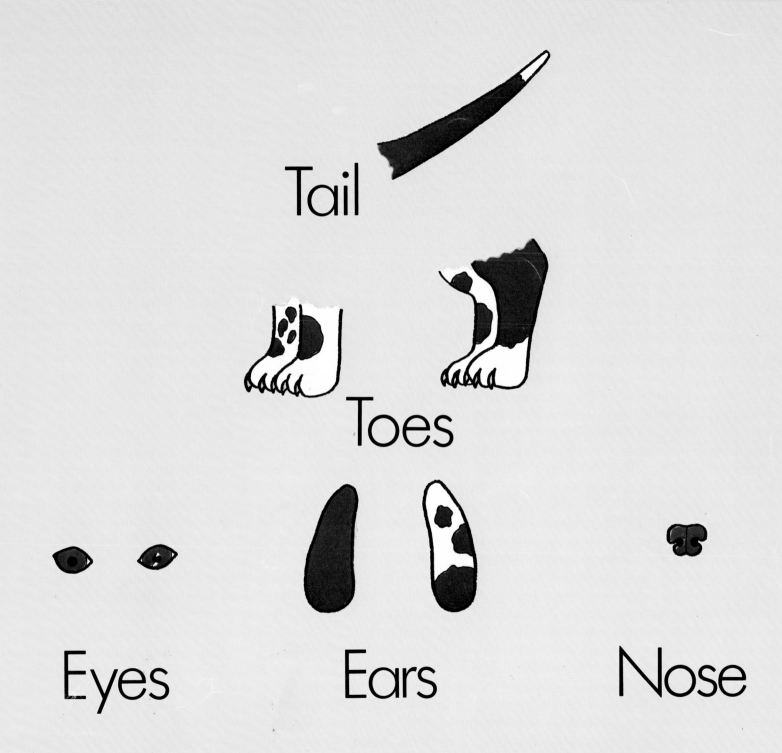

Tail

Toes

Eyes

Ears

Nose

Dog

Tail

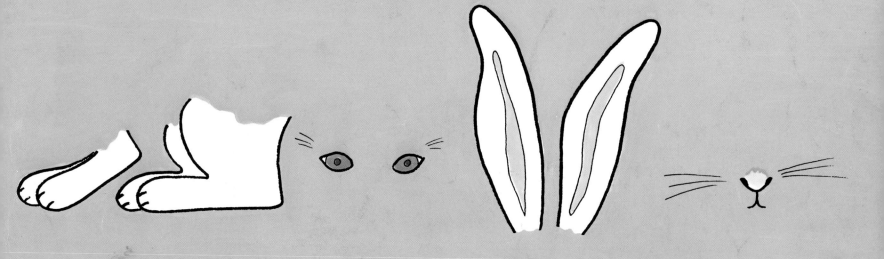

Toes   Eyes   Ears   Nose

Rabbit

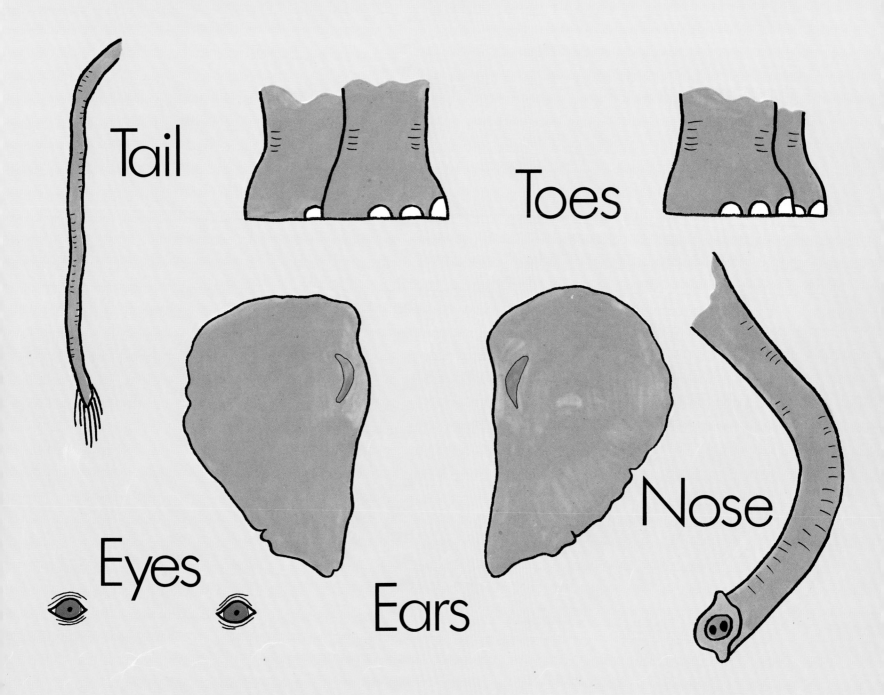

Tail

Toes

Eyes

Ears

Nose

Elephant

Tail   Toes   Eyes   Ears   Nose

(hidden)

Bird

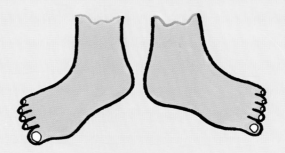

Tail

Toes

Eyes

Ears

Nose

Boy

Tails

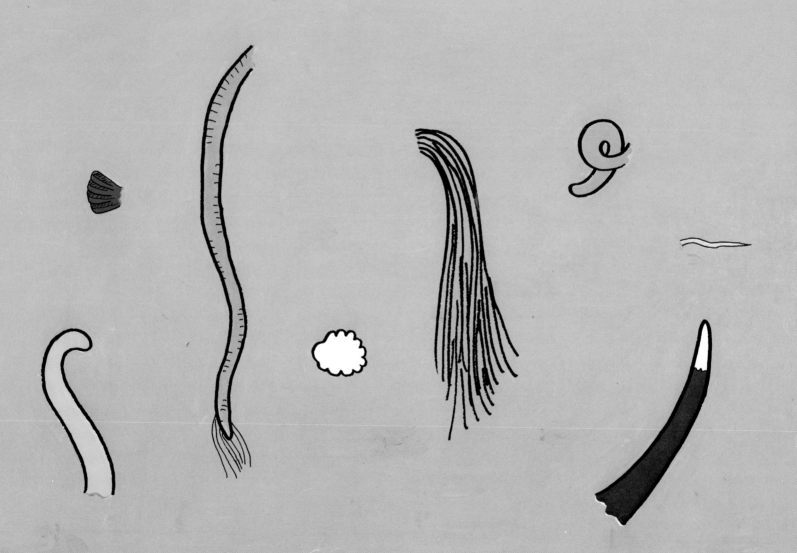

Toes

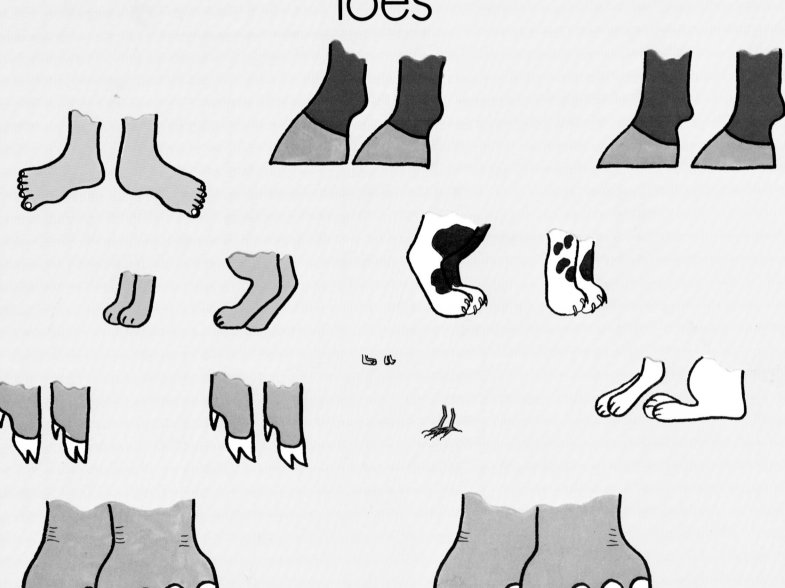

Eyes

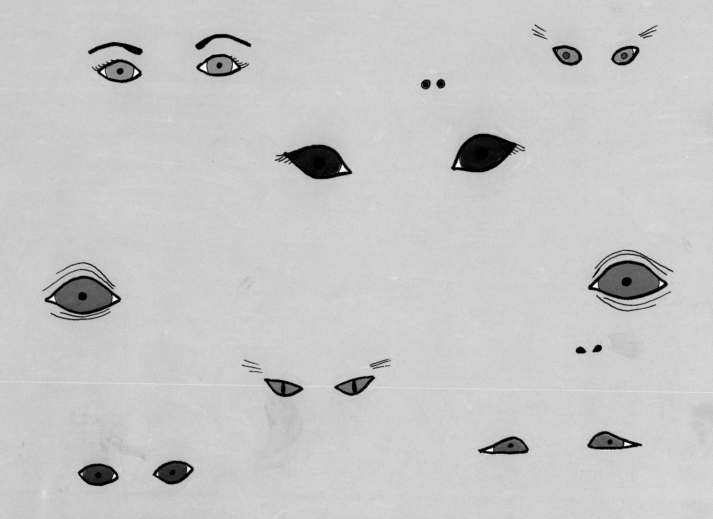

Ears

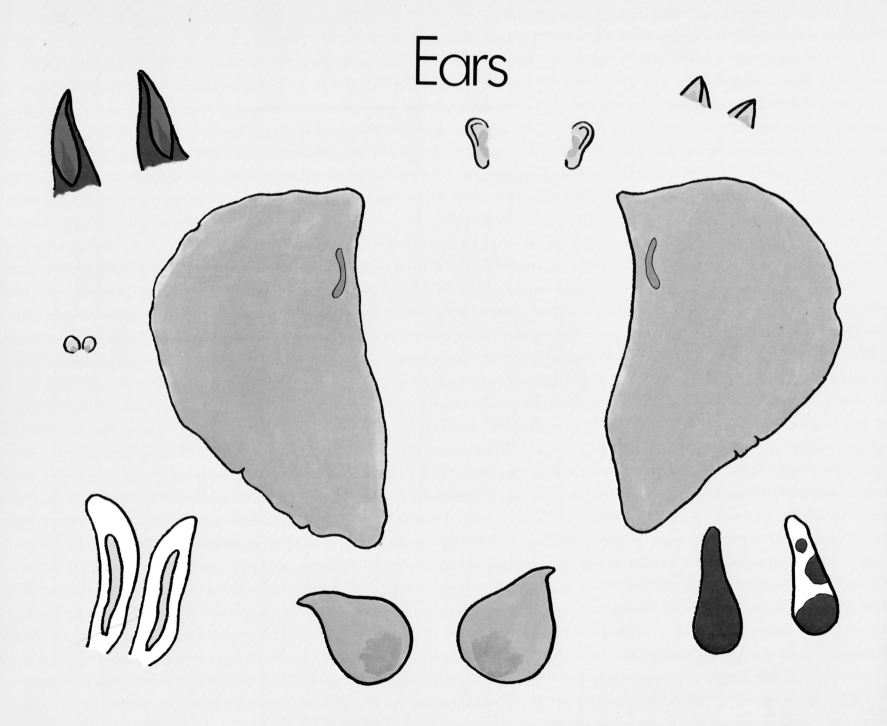

Noses

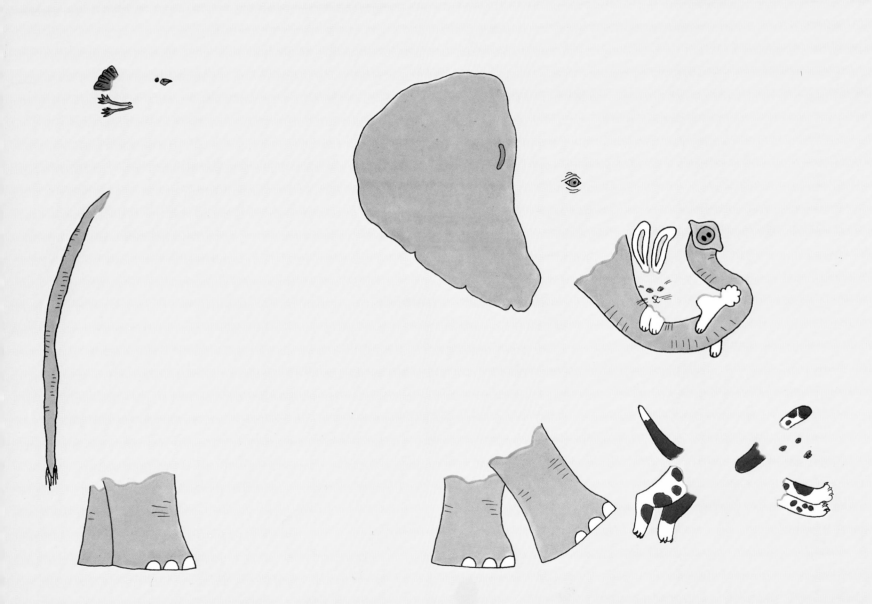